THE FENG SHUI EQUATION

*Formulas to Create Instant Attraction,
Romance & Fame for Single Men & Women*

ABOUT THE AUTHOR

Janice Sugita, has been a practicing feng shui consultant and lecturer for over 12 years and has helped numerous women and men take control of their destiny through the ancient science of Feng Shui. Many of her clients have achieved their goals to increase their personal attraction by following the same simple steps in this book. For over 7 years, she has taken the "peach blossom qi" theories and applied them to "real" people situations with repeated success, first experimenting on herself and then moving onto clients and friends.

With over 25 years of interior design experience, Ms. Sugita has compiled an easy to follow checklist for balancing and enhancing your home using the traditional feng shui principles and philosophies. Using the simplified charts to identify the directions that will enhance one's relationships, health and fame, it is easy to not only produce success in your current home but to use this information wherever you live or work.

Besides lecturing, teaching and contributing to numerous international magazines, Ms. Sugita has appeared as the feng shui expert on several television shows in the past years, including HGTV, Style and Fine Living Channel. She has also traveled extensively for clients to Switzerland, Chile, Buenos Aires, Paris, Brussels and Guadalajara.

Since the public has become more aware of feng shui, she is consulting for national home builders who are interested in providing their buyers communities that have been developed and designed for prosperous and healthy living and are environmentally sane.

This book is dedicated to my loving and talented husband for supporting my efforts to write this book so that many, many others can discover the same possibilities of love that we were fortunate to discover. Without his guidance I would not have been able to conquer the computer and create a serious source of information that would be available worldwide.

Also I would like to thank Master Sang for the invaluable knowledge he has shared with all his students. For me, besides being a great master in feng shui he has been an inspiration and mentor for living life with compassion and respect for all living things.

Lastly, I thank my family for giving me the love that has allowed me to be creative and find my way in life.

Janice Sugita

TABLE OF CONTENTS

INTRODUCTION

Wouldn't you love to wake up and find yourself more desirable and popular? What if strangers suddenly found you irresistible and you didn't have to lose weight, or buy a new wardrobe, change your hairstyle – hmmm.

Opportunity is knocking at your door. We all have the ability to find romance, but we just don't know how. There are many paths to find romance but how do we know which ones will produce the best results? Most of us are unaware that we can use feng shui and energy to enhance the possibilities of romantic encounters and that we can manipulate this path to come straight to our door. In a few easy steps you will be in control of your life and your destiny. Once you take action and begin the process you will be amazed at the results.

FOLLOW ME

Sounds easy and it is. I know, because I tried it myself.

I tested this method before trying it on my clients. Why not? I was available and looking for love. There weren't many places where I felt comfortable to socialize and go out to meet new people so I decided to try this method and see if it really worked. Could I attract new relationships with just flowers? Amazingly, I saw results right away. This is actually the beginning of the story of how I met my husband.

It was a whirlwind romance that began on 2 continents 7000 miles apart and ended up happily married within a year. The story began on a dating website, a couple of years ago when online dating was not yet acceptable but through the miracle of computers we connected. Clearly focused, and with my flowers in place I opened my waiting messages. Two messages – one from England and one from France. I thought the idea of corresponding to someone in another country to be rather ridiculous since we would never meet. I waited a day and finally decided to say hello to the gentleman in France.

Well, amazingly 12 days later I found myself on a plane headed to the south of France. It was the first time using the passport I had obtained almost one year before on Valentine's Day weekend. Of course the only story I could tell my clients and family was that I was going to see a new client who was relocating to the States.

To prepare myself for this decision to travel, I met with a well known couples counselor in Beverly Hills who advised me to go and follow my instincts.

After spending four days in France I found myself one week later waiting at LAX for his arrival to Los Angeles. He never returned to his home in France and we were married one year later, 2 days before Valentine's Day.

This was my first experience using the feng shui method to attract romance, I was a little skeptical in the beginning as you will be but surprised at the results. At first the results might be so subtle that you won't think it is the feng shui but after a couple of times it will be undeniable that you have activated this romance energy. I have tested this method on hundreds of individuals with 99% success with those individuals who actually placed the remedies. The experience of these individuals will be described later in the book.

Once you find that special person, the following chapters will help you further enhance that relationship. Also with these simple tips you can turn your home into a balanced, peaceful environment. You can make major changes in the energy of your home without any construction changes or costs. The result of living in a supportive environment will be success in relationships, finances and health.

I offer this information to all my clients and for anyone interested in finding their perfect mate or for just expanding their social life.

I am confident that if done correctly everyone can achieve their desired results within a very short time. Some of my clients even removed the remedy because they had too many people interested in them too quickly. They couldn't handle so much attention at one time. How many people would love to have that problem?

CHAPTER ONE

USING FENG SHUI
TO ATTRACT
NEW RELATIONSHIPS

WHAT IS FENG SHUI?

Using the knowledge of feng shui, I have been able to transform the lives of my clients and of many other single men and women who have approached me for tips to improve their love life. In the feng shui philosophy, it is believed that we are first controlled by our natural born destiny in life. Then there is luck, feng shui, education and hard work. Only 30% of our life can actually be changed by feng shui, the rest is by our destiny and opportunities.

Basically, feng shui is the science of the observation of the life force energy "qi" in our environment that affects all related aspects of our lives. The literal translation of the Chinese name feng shui is Wind/Water. It represents the air and water currents that moves the universal energy of life called "qi". This "qi" is carried by the air currents and is retained by water.

Traditional or Classical feng shui, originated over 4000 years ago and has nothing to do with superstitions, religion or new age philosophies. Feng shui is based on the observation of the solar system and the affect it has on man and his environment according to orientation and time. The affect can be positive or negative. Living in positive energy attracts prosperity, enhances our health and creates desirable relationships. This positive influence allows us to easily attain our goals for success and healthy living and attracts more creativity, fame and new relationships. It creates an open pathway to achieve those things easily. Negative energy reduces our ability to function at our best and increases the potential for sickness, accidents, delays in finances and success and unhealthy relationships. It puts us in a vulnerable state that does not support our efforts for successful living. Even if you do attain success it will take much more effort and will eventually drain your spirit and energy.

HOW DO WE FIND THIS QI?

We are able to assess this energy or "qi" within our environment/building and manipulate its potential to create the positive results we need to flourish.

In order to analyze the energy in a building we need to calculate the following factors –

1. the time of construction of the building

2. the direction the building/its orientation the surrounding environment

3. the architectural features of the building, interior and exterior

4. the current time/and year

5. the birthdates of the occupants

With this information an experienced feng shui consultant can analyze the exact energy blueprint of a home or office. Unlike the information you read in many "new age" type feng shui books, the energy blueprint for a building can be 1 of 216 different layouts of energy. Besides the initial energy layout, a qualified expert is able to track the continual energy shifts in annual, 20 or 60 year cycles.

I have provided the annual directions in an easy to use chart. There is an annual shift in energy that will influence the occupants in the building. If this new energy "qi" is negative it will reduce the potential for success in prosperity, health and relationships and at the very least make it more difficult to achieve success. Once you have assessed the location of this direction in your home or office you can take the necessary steps to remedy this area accordingly.

Further in the book you will learn the simple ways to assess the "qi" in your surrounding environment and interior architecture. Following the basic principles the "qi" will flow freely into and through the home. With this knowledge you can make the necessary adjustments to create a balanced home that attracts success, fame and romance.

CHAPTER TWO
THE BASIC PRINCIPLES OF FENG SHUI

STARTING WITH BALANCE

One of the most important principles of feng shui is the concept that "qi" or energy is in a constant state of transformation. We call this principle, the Yin/Yang theory. "Everything" in the universe is in a constant cycle of change. It is the eternal order of infinity where one cycle is in transformation into its opposite energy. The actual symbol of the Yin/Yang is called the Tai-ji and in its correct form is shown flowing clockwise, the white at the top representing the most Yang or bright and the black at the bottom symbolizing the most Yin or dark. The basis of this theory includes the cycle of time, seasons, spectrum of colors, temperatures, etc. It is the ever changing balance of light to dark, cold to hot, white to black that influences our lives in order to achieve our level of comfort, productivity and health. The science of feng shui includes the ability to identify and manipulate this energy in our environment that is supportive to our health, prosperity and relationships. It is the art of living in balance in your environment.

HOW DO WE BALANCE THIS QI?

We use only 5 different elements in feng shui to remedy an imbalance of qi. This is called the Five Element Theory. It is treated as a scientific analysis, based on environmental science, physics and mathematics. We do not use any symbolic or superstitious cures or remedies. It does not involve any supernatural or religious beliefs.

The five elements are all forms of the essential qi that make up the universe in some form or another. They are part of the electromagnetic field vibrating at different levels. These different levels of energy take on their own manifestation that is interactive with each other. We look at the potential energy or "qi" that is stored by objects (five element theory) and the continual transformation of this "qi" in cycles (yin/yang theory). To create a balance in energy "qi", these elements must be in this natural productive cycle to provide a supportive environment for the occupants.

The elements are the following:

Fire – Earth – Metal – Water – Wood

Fire – burns and leaves behind ash which in turn creates the earth's layers

Earth – is compressed through the years to form metal

Metal – when it is exposed to the air and temperature forms condensation (water)

Water – is the life source for wood

Wood – creates oxygen and is the fuel for fire

The nature of each element

Because this energy is in constant movement we must adapt our environment accordingly, since not all of the energy will be permanent. Some areas in your home or business will be more positive or negative depending on the current time. In the following chapters you will learn simple feng shui remedies that will positively enhance specific areas in your own home and they include the information for the directions that will be less favorable each year. This will improve your chances for success – a balanced environment not only for romance, but for improved prosperity and health as well.

CHAPTER THREE
TAKE CONTROL

There are different methods using feng shui to activate the areas of your home to attract romance. The first method is to place your bedroom in the area of the home that already has the best potential for romantic energy. The second method is to add water that attracts fame and romance to the directions calculated for your home. Lastly, you can activate romance qi called "peach blossom" with flowers based on your birth information.

BEDROOM IN THE RIGHT DIRECTION

Since you will only be affected by "qi" in the space that you occupy, it is advised that you either move your bedroom to the direction on the chart or place the water feature on the wall of the direction in your bedroom that corresponds to the chart.

Unfortunately, we usually do not have the option to switch bedrooms or build a bedroom in the choice direction so instead we can enhance the "qi" with the placement of the water in the desired direction.

CHAPTER FOUR

WATER FOR ROMANCE, FAME & FORTUNE

When we use water for feng shui it is placed in the direction of the building that needs the element of water to attract and retain this positive "qi" that supports our ability to create romance and prosperity.

I have included a chart that will identify which direction in your home will have this potential for romance, fame and creativity when water is added to the area. This chart is based on the information that is needed to assess the layout of your building. That includes the construction cycle and orientation of the building.

Construction year – is based on the approximate construction year of the building. It is generally when the roof was attached. When the roof is constructed it creates the energy blueprint for the building. Our calculation is based on 20 year cycles, so your neighbor's house may be the same floor plan but if it was built in a different 20 year cycle it will not have the same energy layout. You must calculate the construction year based on the solar calendar. The new year begins on Feb 4-5 for the solar year so if your house was built after Jan 1 and before Feb 4 you use the previous year.

Example – January 19, 2003 you will use the year 2002 for your construction date. If your foundation was poured in December 1963 and the roof installed after Feb 4, 1964 then your construction date will be 1964. The "qi" layout is established once the building is contained.

Orientation of the building – this is the exact compass direction of the sitting direction of the building. Normally the facing of a home is in the front where you have the active, more decorative area. The facing will be the area of the formal rooms like the living and dining rooms. The facing generally has more light and is more active. If your entry door happens to be located on the side of the building that will not necessarily be the facing. The sitting is the heavier, darker side and is usually in the back where the yard is located as well as the utilities, kitchen or family room.

There are specific rules to determine the sitting direction of your space. Using the wrong sitting orientation will give you the wrong direction for the placement of the water.

See drawing for house orientation on pages 28 and 29

The exception for this rule is the home with the ocean or dominant view on the backside. Often times having a lake, golf course or city view can be confusing.

The determining factors for this opposite sitting direction is based on

The dominant view is in the back

The best architectural features are on the backside of the house

The formal living areas and main entry are on the backside

The architect's intent for the front or back will also determine the sitting direction. Houses on the golf course, lake or ocean do not always follow this guideline. Although they have a great view on the backside the front facing on the street side is more architecturally formal and will be the side that you greet your guests.

An example of a building with the backside as the facing would be the homes in Malibu California. along the ocean. The side facing the street usually is more closed with no windows, has the garage facing the street, has a small side entry and has the utility rooms.

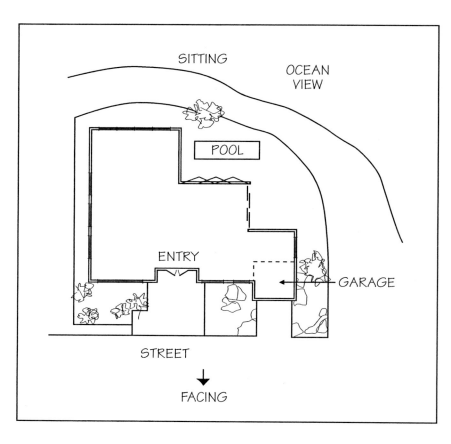

House orientation with the sitting in the back —
ocean view in rear but main formal areas are in the front.

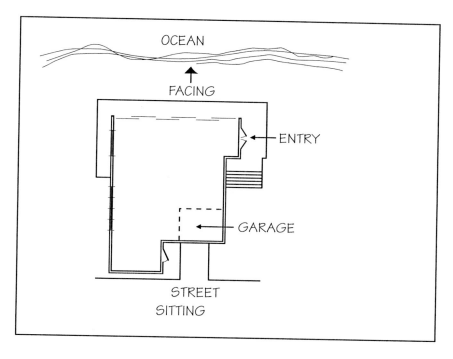

House orientation with the sitting in the front – ocean view in rear with main entry and formal rooms in the rear

Apartments/Condos and Commercial Space

An apartment building will have its own sitting orientation that will be different from the individual unit. The sitting side of the individual unit will be the kitchen or darker unused rooms near the entry door and the formal living room with more windows, patios or balconies will be on the facing side. Also the entry usually will come off of a darker outer hallway or inner courtyard.

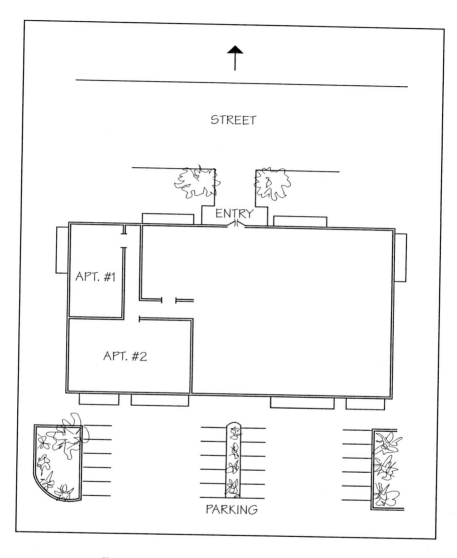

STREET

ENTRY

APT. #1

APT. #2

PARKING

Illustration of typical apartment building

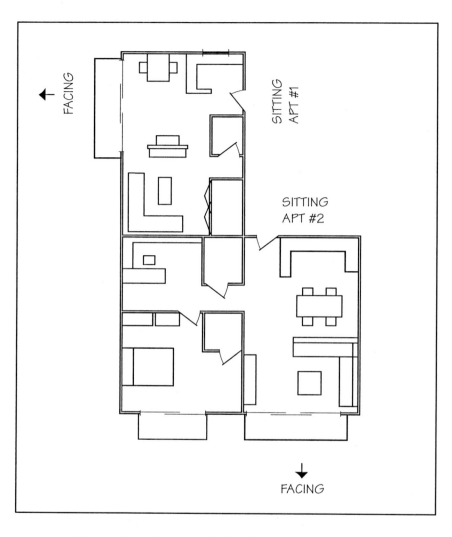

Illustration of typical individual apartment units

*Note the facing of the units correspond to the guidelines
of facing and sitting orientation

Once you have established the sitting/facing of your home, construction year and have taken an exact compass reading you will be able to look at this chart and see the directions that are inherently supportive to romance and fame. These directions are delineated by 15 degrees and are very exact. By placing moving water in these directions you will attract and enhance this qi.

The following guidelines will help you achieve these positive results –

The amount of water needed is in proportion to the size of the space. 5% of the sq. footage of the space equals the gallons of water required. An average room can use between 1-5 gallons of water.

When water is needed outside, the minimum amount of water can vary from 40-100 gallons depending on the sq. ft. of the building.

Water must be clean and moving, a pump is necessary

The container must be uncovered so the water interacts with the "qi".

The earth element reduces the amount of water so using a ceramic or stone container filled with stones will lessen the affect of the water. Metal containers are more supportive to the water. This is important in areas where the space for water is limited

The water does not need fish or any decoration nor are the fish beneficial to the results.

Adding an ultraviolet light element or reverse osmosis feature will attract and destroy airborne bacteria and viruses. This feature is helpful but not necessary

Recently healthcare, hospitality and commercial facilities have discovered the positive attributes of interior water features for improving health and well being, mentally and physically. The current research shows the addition of a water feature will reoxygenate and renew interior air "qi". This renewal of air "qi" is currently being researched for the benefits to mental and physical health. This is especially beneficial for those working or living in enclosed buildings.

Placing the water

First choice – would be to place the water in the bedroom that corresponds to that direction.

Second choice – would to place the water in the entry or another room that you occupy for long periods of time.

Third choice – would be to place the water next to the wall in your bedroom that corresponds to the best direction.

Source for fountains

Accents in Water has custom contemporary metal water features with a new line of feng shui fountains. The materials and sizes of these fountains are designed for use with traditional feng shui principles described in this book. These fountains are also available with the UV and osmosis filters. I have designed these water features to fulfill the requirements necessary for feng shui and they can be purchased on my website – www.jssugita.com.

WATER DIRECTION CHARTS

BEST DIRECTIONS FOR WATER

SITTING NORTH

	337.5-352.5	352.5-7.5	7.5-22.5
1864-1883	SE, W	E, NW	E, NW
1884-1903	SW, W	E, NE	E, NE
1904-1923	S, SW	NE, N	NE, N
1924-1943	S	N	N
1944-1963	S, NE	SE, N	SE, N
1964-1983	E, NE	SW, W	SW, W
1984-2003	E, NW	SE, W	SE, W
2004-2023	NW	SE	SE
2024-2043	SE	NW	NW

*Placing water in the NE direction during 2004-2023 may increase the potential for romance but may reduce the potential for prosperity.

BEST DIRECTIONS FOR WATER

SITTING NORTH EAST

	22.5-37.5	37.5-52.5	52.5-67.5
1864-1883	SW	NE	NE
1884-1903	S, NW	SE, N	SE, N
1904-1923	S, W	E, N	E, N
1924-1943	SW, NE	NE, SW	NE, SW
1944-1963	S, E	N, W	N, W
1964-1983	S, NW	SE, W	SE, W
1984-2003	NE	SW	SW
2004-2023	E, NW	SE, W	SE, W
2024-2043	W, NW	SE, E	SE, E

BEST DIRECTIONS FOR WATER

SITTING EAST

	62.5-82.5	82.5-97.5	97.5-112.5
1864-1883	S, NW	SE, N	SE, N
1884-1903	S	N	N
1904-1923	SE, NE	SW, NW	SW, NW
1924-1943	E, W	W, E	W, E
1944-1963	SW, NW	SE, NE	SE, NE
1964-1983	S	N	N
1984-2003	SE, S	S, NW	S, NW
2004-2023	W, NE	E, SW	E, SW
2024-2043	SW, E	NE, W	NE, W

BEST DIRECTIONS FOR WATER

SITTING SOUTH EAST

	112.5-127.5	127.5-142.5	142.65-157.5
1864-1883	S, E	W, N	W, N
1884-1903	NE, NW	SW, SE	SW, SE
1904-1923	E	W	W
1924-1943	NW	SE	SE
1944-1963	W	E	E
1964-1983	SW, NW	SE, NE	SE, NE
1984-2003	S, W	E, N	E, N
2004-2023	S, SW	NE, N	NE, N
2024-2043	S, NE	N, SW	N, SW

BEST DIRECTIONS FOR WATER

SITTING SOUTH

	157.5-172.5	172.5-187.5	187.5-202.5
1864-1883	SE, W	E, NW	E, NW
1884-1903	SW, W	E	E, NE
1904-1923	S, SW	NE, N	NE, N
1924-1943	S	S	S
1944-1963	S, NE	SW, W	SW, W
1964-1983	E, NE	SW, W	SW, W
1984-2003	E, NW	SE, W	SE, W
2004-2023	NW	SE	SE
2024-2043	SE	NW	NW

BEST DIRECTIONS FOR WATER

SITTING SOUTH WEST

	202.5-217.5	217.5-232.5	232.5-247.5
1864-1883	SW	NE	NE
1884-1903	S, NW	SE, N	SE, N
1904-1923	S, W	E, N	E, N
1924-1943	NE, SW	SW, NE	SW, NE
1944-1963	S, E	W, S	W, S
1964-1983	S, NW	SE, N	SE, N
1984-2003	NE	SW	SW
2004-2023	E, NW	SE, W	SE, W
2024-2043	W, NW	SE, E	SE, E

BEST DIRECTIONS FOR WATER

SITTING NORTH WEST

	292.5-307.5	307.5-322.5	322.5-337.5
1864-1883	S, E	W, N	W, N
1884-1903	NW, NE	SW, SE	SW, SE
1904-1923	E	W	W
1924-1943	NW	SE	SE
1944-1963	W	E	E
1964-1983	SW, NW	SE, NE	SE, NE
1984-2003	S, W	E, N	E, N
2004-2023	SW	NE, N	NE, N
2024-2043	S, NE	SW, N	SW, N

In the following chapters you will learn even more ways to improve your home or business yourself by analyzing the outside environment, location, architecture and applying the basic principles of feng shui. Most feng shui principles are the same as basic interior design principles. Choose the correct colors, textures and styles that make you feel comfortable and keep the lighting and space in balance.

Many of the principles of feng shui are based on keeping the balance in our life. This also applies to our surroundings and our personal energy and lifestyle. Not only will you be able to improve your surroundings to attract romance but you can increase your personal energy that will make you feel more energized and attractive. We can use this balance to simplify our lifestyle and live with less stress.

It has been proven that stress is one of the main reasons for the reduction of the immune system that causes sickness and disease.

CHAPTER FIVE

PEACH BLOSSOM QI

The easiest and fastest method to enhance romantic energy is to use a simple formula that has remained a secret of feng shui masters. It is based on Chinese astrological and feng shui observations throughout the centuries. This special formula activates the energy that attracts romance and is individualized according to your birth year and can work within 24 hours.

"Peach blossom" is the Chinese term for romantic energy. It is the energy of a blossoming new love or relationship. The term peach blossom is a symbol of love that blossoms in the spring with the flowering trees. Unlike the water feature which will attract the fame and romance to that particular area, the peach blossom formula will bring this attraction only to the person of that birth year. You will identify peach blossom energy in your home and learn how to activate this energy and make it work for you. This method utilizes your year of birth and assigns a particular color flower and color vase that is based on your birth information. The flower/vase combination is placed in an exact direction of your home or bedroom to become activated. It is very successful and can work as quickly as a day to one week. I have proven this method with much success with clients of all ages, backgrounds and gender preference. The ultimate goal in activating this romance energy is to bring new opportunities to blossom into lasting and happy relationships.

CHAPTER SIX

THE FLOWER AND VASE FORMULA

1. Follow the chart to find your **birth date** – note the correct direction and corresponding flower color and vase color. Use only fresh flowers for this formula, preferably no dyed flowers. The color of the blossom should be the dominant color of the flower. The flowers should be free of dirt, kept in clean water and changed when wilted if you want to continue the desired effect. The flowers must be a budding species that can blossom, hence the "peach blossom" name. Greenery and potted plants will not work. It is best to check the flower chart and choose the flower that will last the longest. I found the results were more positive when more than one flower was used. I suggest using at least 6 stems to be effective.

2. It is important to use a vase that holds a significant amount of water and has a large mouth opening. The size of the vase will determine the amount of water. Small mouth or bottle neck vases tend to constrict the positive effect of the flowers and are not recommended. The material of the vase is not as important as the overall color. The color of the container must correspond to your flower color. The container can be glass, ceramic, metal or plastic. A clear glass or plastic container can be used if you add the glass pebbles in the corresponding color. If you do not see immediate results you may want to switch to a vase of a solid color.

3. Once you find the corresponding flower and color vase, use a compass to locate the direction for placement. A compass reading should be taken outside the building in order to get an accurate reading. The metal structure of a building or furnishings can distort your reading. Keep the compass waist high and avoid standing next to any cars or any underground power sources. Heavy metal belts, watches or other jewelry can also affect the accuracy of your reading. Double check your reading by standing in 2 or 3 different locations. It is important not to guess at the direction without a compass.

4. I have found the best results by placing the flowers in the best direction in your bedroom. The room or area should not be cluttered or dark. The flowers should be in a healthy, positive, well ventilated and well lit environment and should be replaced once it shows signs of wilting. *See the bedroom layout on page 59.*

Trimming the stems of the flowers and adding additives such as aspirin or drops of bleach to the water will prolong the life of the flower. This formula works in an apartment or mansion. In this case "size does not matter". But it is advisable to follow the other chapters in the book to help create an environment that is supportive to positive relationships. It is easier to attract healthy and happy people for new relationships if you feel healthy and happy.

5. Make sure you are mentally and physically available once you place the flowers. You may see results the first day! An important detail, encounters may be very subtle and random so don't expect the man or woman of your dreams to appear immediately. This method will give you a lot of choices. It is up to you to choose the right one.

COUPLES BEWARE

Be careful if you are currently in a relationship. Trying this formula may cause difficulties in that relationship once you place the flowers. It is not advisable to try this if you are not sure that you want to end the relationship. It is not recommended for increasing romance in an existing marriage or relationship because it can bring a third party into the picture as well as making the couple more attracted to each other. It is possible that it will create more passion between the couple but it may be one sided if the other is getting attention from outside parties. It may be effective to spark relationships if it makes both parties feel reenergized and desirable.

PEACH BLOSSOM DIRECTION CHART

The following birthdates are based on the Chinese New Year's dates that begin on February 4 and 5. If you were born before this date then you would refer to the previous year.

Example – January 15, 2004 year would still remain 2003

Example – February 1, 1944 year would still remain 1943

West	1900	1912	1924	1936	1948	1960	1972	1984	1996
South	1901	1913	1925	1937	1949	1961	1973	1985	1997
East	1902	1914	1926	1938	1950	1962	1974	1986	1998
North	1903	1915	1927	1939	1951	1963	1975	1987	1999
West	1904	1916	1928	1940	1952	1964	1976	1988	2000
South	1905	1917	1929	1941	1953	1965	1977	1989	2001
East	1906	1918	1930	1942	1954	1966	1978	1990	2002
North	1907	1919	1931	1943	1955	1967	1979	1991	2003
West	1908	1920	1932	1944	1956	1968	1980	1992	2004
South	1909	1921	1933	1945	1957	1969	1981	1993	2005
East	1910	1922	1934	1946	1958	1970	1982	1994,	2006
North	1911	1923	1935	1947	1959	1971	1983	1995	2007

The exact compass direction is needed in this method. If possible use the center of the direction for best results.

West — 262.5-277.5

South — 172.5-167.5

East — 82.5-97.5

North — 352.5-7.5

DIRECTION, COLOR AND VASE CHART

WEST DIRECTION

FLOWER COLOR – White flowers, can have a center of color but must be predominately white or ivory

VASE COLOR – White, silver, gold color

SOUTH DIRECTION

FLOWER COLOR – Red, purple, dark pink

VASE COLOR – Red, purple, dark pink

EAST DIRECTION

FLOWER COLOR – Green

VASE COLOR – Green

NORTH DIRECTION

FLOWER COLOR – Blue

VASE COLOR – Blue or black

FLOWER SELECTION CHART

Your selection of flowers will vary depending on the season. Most of the flowers I have suggested are more generic and can be found year round. The color red can be substituted for pink or purple. The irises range from blue to purple. If you use an iris for a blue color and you have no response, try a different blue flower, the color may be too purple.

It is best to add a preservative to the water to prolong the freshness of the flower. A few drops of household bleach will also keep the water from forming bacteria. An average flower should last about a week. Orchids will last 2 to 3 weeks with clean water. For all flowers trim the ends of the stems about 2 inches every other day and place back into clean water. Once they have wilted they must be changed it you want to continue the results.

BLUE
Delphiniums, range from blue to violet, same for irises (check the shade), hydrangeas

RED/PINK
Roses, tulips, carnations, gerberas, peonies

PURPLE
Purple dendrobium orchids, some irises

GREEN

Miniature pin cushion mums, green dendrobium orchids, belles of Ireland

WHITE

Roses, lilies, carnations, daisies, tulips, orchids, anemones, narcissus, sweet pea, calla lilies, white orchids

VASE SELECTION

Your vase can be any design or style as long as it doesn't have a narrow neck opening and it holds a lot of water. With a large mouth vase the water will be able to interact with the "qi". In remedies for feng shui where water is needed for increasing prosperity we say you want the water to be equivalent to amount of money you want to make. If you add a little you will only make a little. The same is for the peach blossom.

I don't suggest using any bud vases as they are too small and do not hold enough water or flowers. The water helps to generate this new attraction energy, so add a lot!

SHAPE OF THE VASE

ROUND BALL – this is good as long as the mouth is wide

SQUARE – good shape

TALL CYLINDRICAL – good shape

BULB SHAPE – not good if mouth is small or bottleneck

V SHAPE – good if it holds enough water

SHALLOW CURVE – only useful if it is not too flat

COLOR OF VASE

The color can be a painted finish, glass, metal or plastic. If you use a clear glass vase then colored glass rocks can be used. Make sure you fill the vase with a proportionate amount of pebbles to the size of the vase to add the color.

White – for West can be white or a metallic material like brass or silver

Blue – for North can be blue or black

Green – can be any shade from fluorescent green to olive

Red – can be used in different shades of red, purple, or pink. If you use a light pink and have no response it could be your pink was too light. Red is an activating color and a light pink may not be as effective. Since red is an activating color it can also activate negative qi in that space. Look on the yearly chart to see if your direction will not be affected by the introduction of red or purple.

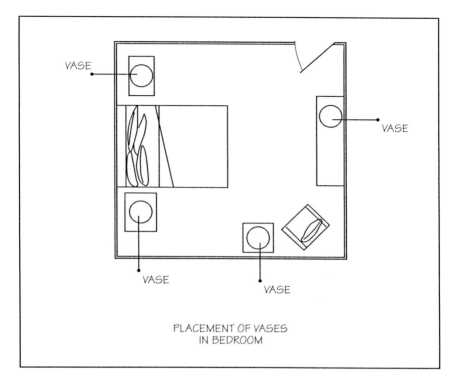

Illustration of different locations for vase

PLACEMENT OF VASE IN ROOM

- First choice for vase placement will be in bedroom.

- The vase must be placed in the correct direction

- The vase does not have to be located next to the bed

- Vase works best if placed in the center of the required direction

READING THE COMPASS

Unless you grew up a boy scout you will probably not be familiar with using a compass. You can buy a compass at your local sporting good store in the camping section. The price will vary between $5.00 to 45.00. All of them work on the same principle but the more elaborate ones have view finders for mapping destinations. Not necessary for our purpose. Just make sure the compass face has the individual increments for 360 degrees.

Here are a couple of simple steps to take a correct reading.

1. Stand outside your home or apartment with your back to the front of the building. For this introductory type of reading it is not necessary to determine the sitting or facing of the building. You just need to set a point to determine the directions of the building. Avoid standing next to cars, electrical sources or multilevel parking structures. If you live in the middle of high rise structures you will have to walk to an open area away from the metal structures to get an accurate reading. In a city like New York you may have to walk several streets away to an open lot. Make sure the street is parallel to your building.

2. Hold the compass waist high and level

3. Look around at the environment to be sure there are no other objects that can distort your reading.

4. Take a reading in several different areas, front, back and sides.

5. If you live in an apartment the facing direction may be different from the building's entrance. *See page 31 and 32 for more instructions.*

POSITIONING YOURSELF TO USE THE COMPASS

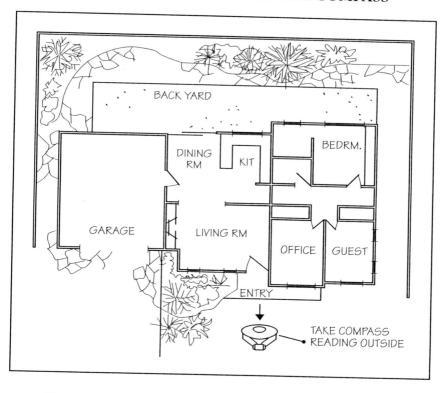

Illustration for the correct way to take a compass reading

CHAPTER SEVEN

WHAT TO EXPECT – RANDOM ENCOUNTERS & EX'S

Once you place the flowers in the correct direction you can start seeing results the same day. I have had many clients say that they had an immediate response. Since this is a random attraction you can expect the unexpected.

Here are a few examples:

1. You may find yourself being approached at the grocery store, restaurants, school, workplace, gym or anywhere. It could be an interaction between people that you happen to pass or maybe have seen you before or have just decided to approach you in conversation.

2. Friends or relatives may suddenly set you up on a double or blind date

3. Ex boyfriends or girlfriends can call out of the blue with renewed interest, even if you are no longer interested

4. Acquaintances may find you more attractive and give you more attention

5. Someone you may have met or dated years ago may suddenly call again

You can also experience something unusual, for example:

– A female student of mine worked as a cashier in a restaurant. After placing the flowers she had a man come in and place a turquoise bracelet on her wrist and left without even introducing himself.

– Another student who was a waitress had a customer who left his phone number on several sugar packets.

– One of my clients reported that she received flowers for her birthday from an ex boyfriend she had not seen for 2 years even though it wasn't her birthday.

– There are some drawbacks – it can attract the married as well as singles. I had one woman who was pursued by her married boss.

BE ON THE LOOKOUT

The key is to be observant and do not discount any encounter. Some people think that just because they aren't attracted to that particular person that it is not working. An important point to remember is that it is random and it will give you a lot of options. But always be cautious when meeting new people and act in a safe manner. It's always best to be safe and treat strangers accordingly. Stay in public spaces and be aware of your surroundings. It will be important to screen out those you find undesirable.

DON'T FORGET FAME AND FORTUNE

The peach blossom qi also enhances the potential for fame especially in the entertainment field and the arts. It is identified as the same energy as romance and can be activated by the same methods with flowers or with water. Many of my clients in the entertainment field unknowingly will choose a home with a great deal of creative qi. Their fame and creativity can be increased by activating the right directions with water and the flower method. Again this potential increases popularity and it will come from different sources.

WORKS FOR EVERYONE

In my opinion the peach blossom formula works for everyone! Age, sex or sexual preference does not matter. I found 99% success on women and men between the ages of 19 to 60. Many women over 50 had as much success as the 20 year olds. I didn't have anyone over 60 interested to try but that doesn't mean it wouldn't work as well.

The women and men came from all different lifestyles and demographics. They were single or divorced and in all different heights and weights.

THE "A" LIST

Some attractive men and women originally reported they didn't notice much change until I reviewed the events of their week. These individuals were so used to being approached that they were expecting dramatic changes and events so they dismissed the usual whistles, stares and come on lines. One good looking male client said he didn't notice any difference the first couple of days.

The second week he called me and said "the women in his office were acting so provocative towards him that it was almost porno-graphic". He was used to the usual flirting but the advances from the women were becoming increasingly competitive and physical to get his attention.

Another male client who was very shy tried the flowers and had a woman ask him out on a date the same week.

STRAIGHT, GAY AND THE CONFUSED

One of my students who is a young gay male waited until the third week of class to finally try the flowers. He came to class that week and told everyone that the first day of placing the flowers he received calls from an older man who called continuously that week until he finally threw the flowers away. He thought the attraction was too overwhelming especially since he was not attracted to this man.

Even if you aren't gay it is possible to get attention from either sex. A female client said she received definite attention from an-other female in her class after she placed the flowers.

GENERATION X

For younger women and men in their 20's, the experience varied according to their availability. Many of these women had more flirtatious encounters but found them more random and less serious. Most of these same women were students who worked at part time jobs that dealt with the public. Some of their en-counters involved patrons interacting with them on the job. Most females were approached by people they didn't know and some by old boyfriends.

Besides attention from the opposite sex, I had a male client who reported that besides attention from females, all his friends wanted to meet at his house and have barbeques and parties, which never happened before. His friends also started to set him up on blind dates.

BABY B's

> *"The trouble with the rat race is that even if you win, you're still a rat"*
> LILY TOMLIN

I think the baby boomers are the real Generation "EX." Ex wives and ex husbands and ex –cuses. Some of my clients who received this info did not act on it because they felt it wasn't the right time. Usually the kid's activities came first or they were finishing a project or were leaving town, etc, etc. The most fantastic part of the peach blossom is that it works now! So how long are you going to say that it would be nice to meet someone new but do nothing to act on it?

The women I know who participated had results very quickly. It took about an average of 1 to 2 days to get a response from the flowers. Their ages ranged from 37-55 years old and their experiences were mostly random encounters from new acquaintances and ex boyfriends.

Sample of actual experiences taken
from written survey of participants

"A guy I was dating told me he loved me and my ex showed up on my front door. Also, a guy I met on the subway in December asked me out."

"My ex-boyfriend started calling and one unwanted friend continuously came over"

"I met a man who gave me wonderful compliments but I found out he was married."

"After I removed the flowers I felt there was still a lot of attention towards me. I met my girlfriend, and her male friend basically propositioned me within the first 5 minutes of meeting and we proceeded to have a perfect day together. I also had a girl proposition me which was strange".

"People just came up to me and said "hi" and also past friends would randomly bump into me."

"In one day 3 men approached me, 2 at the mall and one while I was driving. I cut this guy off on the road, then he yelled "you're beautiful" and I thought he was really cute. We pulled over to meet and it turned out to be my ex-boyfriends friend from 4 years ago who I always had a crush on but he had a girlfriend at the same time."

"During the week I met a surfer from Hawaii and a guy from Phoenix."

CHAPTER EIGHT
FINDING MR. RIGHT

"The first step to getting the things you want out of life is this; decide what you want"
BEN STEIN

Mr. or Ms Who?

How do we find Mr. Right if we don't know what we're looking for? Creating a list is helpful to identify that perfect person when he or she comes along. The peach blossom formula will bring you many different people into your life but it is up to you to be selective. By establishing this list you will eliminate those that do not fit and you will continue in the direction which will bring you more success. Not recognizing your incompatibility is like trying on clothes and not checking the size. Would you go shopping for clothes and try on any size or would you look for the size and style that fits you? Do you have the same taste that you had 10 or 15 years ago? Probably not. As we grow and mature it is important to acknowledge that our tastes are also changing. Think about what it is you want and declare it – don't just wish for it to happen.

BE CAREFUL WHAT YOU WISH FOR...

"Complaining is good for you as long as you're not complaining to the person you're complaining about"
LYNN JOHNSON

The perfect mate is possible to find but not to create. Most times we make life more difficult by trying to turn our mate into someone that fits or expectations. This is a relationship destined to doom.

An important principle in feng shui is to "simplify your life". Why not decide what characteristics you want in this person and then go out and find it rather than try to change someone. It is the same idea as deciding to buy a car. Once you decide on the model, color and extras, suddenly you start seeing that car everywhere. The peach blossom formula will bring many opportunities into your life. It is up to you to choose which relationships are worth pursuing. Your list should be memorized or placed in a visible location that will be a constant reminder for you.

I believe in the idea of putting your thoughts into the universe. This thought process increases the chances of finding Mr. Right. The list should consist of the physical characteristics, personality attributes, hobbies, interests and career. Asking for a particular individual to appear is not helpful and not probable. Most importantly, this list helps us focus on the desired attributes of this person. It is easy to be swept away by first impressions that do not really correspond to our true desires.

> *"Sexiness wears thin after a while and beauty fades,*
> *but to be married to a man who makes you*
> *laugh every day, ah, now that's a treat."*
> JOANNE WOODARD – WIFE OF PAUL NEWMAN

This list will help you in your quest for a successful relationship. It works! Yes, make the list, being very specific for the characteristics of your ideal partner. I have provided a sample -

1. age

2. height and weight

3. color of eyes and hair

4. hobbies and interests

5. occupation

6. personality and special qualities something special that you want from this person that you haven't found before

Memorize this list or place it in a location that is visible to "only" you. It will serve as a reminder once you start meeting new people. It is especially helpful as a reminder if you are approached by an ex. If he or she is not on your list then it is best to pass on the relationship. I always tell my clients to be careful what you wish for. Of course this is not feng shui but it helps to create a more successful relationship that can be enhanced using the feng shui tips.

Now that you have established your goal, it is possible to focus on what you need to do to accomplish it.

1. Make your list

2. Memorize and declare it

3. Focus on the path to your goal

4. Act quickly; the flowers work very fast

READY OR NOT

"Action may not always bring happiness;
but there is no happiness without action".

Sometimes we avoid relationships unconsciously because we aren't ready for Mr. or Ms. Right. We make excuses that after we lose 10 lbs we'll be ready or after Christmas we will have more time, excuses, excuses. Perfect example – in one of my classes I had 20 students. The first week 18 students eagerly asked to participate in my peach blossom study. At the end of 2 weeks, only 1 person had actually gone out to purchase the flowers and vase. Results in 4 weeks – only 3 more had participated in the study. Yet all 4 had experienced positive results. My conclusion is that we complain that we can't find relationships but we don't make the effort! The peach blossom formula does not wait for you to lose 10 lbs. It works now! Irregardless of your faults or excuses, it works. So there is no reason not to begin the process today!

LOOKING FOR LOVE IN ALL THE WRONG PLACES

"Opportunities are like sunsets,
if you wait too long, you miss them"
UNKNOWN

It doesn't matter if you are looking for quantity or quality, being available is important. These new people must be able to find you. If you are holed up in your room night after night watching television, your chances of finding that right person will be reduced.

1. Expand your surroundings, check your list and join clubs, classes or organizations where you would find someone who enjoys the same interests.

2. Change your routine, try different restaurants, take up a new sport, create an adventure trip or do something new. Otherwise you will end up meeting the same type of people that are not on your list.

3. Be aware of your surroundings and the people around you.

4. Walk or run in a 5k, walk your dog or go chase a Frisbee.

5. Go to a concert or sporting event.

6. Check your local listings for festivals, art openings, and conventions.

7. Check the internet, join a dating website.

"Never frown even when you are sad, because you never know when someone is falling in love with your smile"
UNKNOWN

Allow yourself to be approachable. It is important to make eye contact and remember you can't hurt anyone with a smile. Of course we should always be safe and protect ourselves accordingly. Don't leave with someone you don't know just because they are friendly. Be safe and smart!

WOULD YOU FIND YOURSELF
ON HIS OR HER LIST?

"Don't be yourself, be superior to the fellow you were yesterday"
AUTHOR UNKNOWN

Do you expect the man or woman of your dreams to be good looking, intelligent, funny, athletic, sensitive, etc. What about you? Is your character up to par?

LADIES

Have the years of independence and the competitive workplace enhanced or depleted your sensitive, feminine nature? Perhaps inside we are still vulnerable and cute but this is not who's answering the phone in the business place.

In my classes I had the students fill out a questionnaire with a rating system of how they viewed themselves and of the person they hoped to find. I found most females to be pretty conservative in their expectations, no one was looking for the perfect 10.

Luckily we live in a time when 40's are the new 30's. Women are looking better everyday as well as "feeling" more positive about who they are. Don't be afraid to dream, just be fair and ask yourself "would you be on his list as well ?" If not, then ask what do I need to change to make that happen. You may have more chances of success of finding that person who fits your category.

"The biggest room in the world is the room for improvement"
UNKNOWN

MEN – BEAUTY AND THE BEAST?

According to all the advertisements on TV and magazines it seems men are generally looking for the younger more attractive female, that physical beauty is somewhat of a requirement. But if you analyzed your needs and were really specific about your list for Ms. Right you might see some additional qualities besides youth and beauty. These are the qualities that have to surpass the first couple of dates. You need to be able to keep the interest once the physical side gets old. It is nice to be in a relationship with someone with whom you can share your interests. Rather than be with someone who is only attracted to you because of the interests you own, like sports cars, boats, etc. Are they with you for who you are, or for what you have or represent?

Middle aged crisis? Perhaps this is your dilemma.

I wonder if the younger men actually sit down and think about what qualities might be important. As youth slips by and you start that balding process it could more than what's in your wallet that's needed to attract that perfect person. Men with a sense of humor, sensitivity and chivalry can be more valuable than gold.

YOU ARE THE NEW PRIORITY

Many times the "baby boomers" have put their love life on hold because they just don't have time. Between kid's schedules, and career commitments their personal life takes a back seat. Where do you fit on your list of priorities?

1. Do you spend most of your time after work driving your children to their activities?

2. Do you belong to any clubs or organizations besides work or kids?

3. Have you spent much time pursuing any new hobbies

4. Where do you go to spend some alone time?

5. When was the last time you went on a date ?

If you fit into this category your chances of success will increase if you allow yourself to be more spontaneous, loosen control and change your routine. I found that the women and men who had less success didn't want anything or anyone to change their routine. Also, I have noted that the same people were less likely to replace the wilted flowers. The more" successful " participants were more open to any results and actually made an effort to meet new people.

Using the feng shui principles we want to create a harmonious balance in all our relationships. To live in harmony with our family and romantic relationships it helps to get our environment in order. Feeling balanced, de-stressed and healthy are key to any successful relationship. Remember the term, "feeling good in our skin"? It refers to being happy with yourself before you can be happy with others.

You will learn some tips to reduce the "shas" or negative influences in your environment and enhance the positive "qi" energy that will help support your goals for balanced living. Follow these tips to keep your new relationships happy and successful.

CHAPTER NINE

MAKING YOUR HOME HEALTHY – NEUTRALIZE THE NEGATIVES

Neutralize negative shas. "Shas" in feng shui terminology are negative energies that affect our physical and mental health. Different exterior or interior architectural features of a building will create negative influences that causes invisible energy to be harmful to our health. Balancing the energy within and around our home will keep it more productive for us to be able to create those great relationships and prosperity.

EXTERIOR

There are easy and basic methods for analyzing and improving the energy potential of your home.

Take a look at the exterior first and follow these easy steps:

1. Examine the property around your home. Start from the front of the building and observe if there are any neighboring buildings with sharp corners or architectural features pointing directly at your entry.

Trees or large boulders can absorb and establish a buffer for this type of negative energy. Trim back any overgrown trees or shrubberies that block your entry or over shadow the light entering the windows. If the interior of a building is too dark, it is considered too "yin" (negative) and is not desirable or healthy.

2. The location of a building is important –

Avoid areas with negative and unhealthy energy such as hospitals, cemeteries, and toxic dumps. Fire and police stations have energy that is too "Yang" or active because of the sirens and the activity of responding to crisis and crime.

If you live in a multi-storied apartment, avoid the units on the floor right above the parking structure. The constant movement of metal energy is not healthy.

Smaller buildings that are surrounded by taller multistoried buildings will make the occupants feel dominated and can cause depression.

The support of a building is important to keep financially healthy and to make the occupants feel supported. Buildings at the top of a hill with no support will be difficult for occupants to keep their money.

Also houses built on a stilt foundation are not good for families or relationships. This missing support under the building makes the occupants feel unstable.

3. Electrical transformers, power lines and any machinery with concentrations of electromagnetic energy can affect our health.

Placing a buffer such as large boulders or rocks between the source and your home will help absorb the harmful electrical energy. This is especially important when the transformers are near a bedroom. The earth element will absorb this energy to prevent it from entering the building.

4. Water is an important element in feng shui and can be supportive to enhance energy for romance and finances, if used correctly.

To activate this energy water must be clean and moving. Some feng shui books suggest adding fish to the water. Fish can be decorative and can be included but the presence of fish does not change or add energy.

When water is needed as a remedy for feng shui, the quantity must be in proportion to the size of the building. Women can also add water in the southeast direction of their bedroom to enhance the peach blossom energy.

The placement of water to increase this potential can be determined by a feng shui consultant. For our purposes of enhancing the peach blossom energy I have provided a chart. This chart identifies the direction to be activated according to the sitting direction of your building and construction date. It is important to follow the steps correctly in order to identify the direction for your home.

5. Street location

The movement of the qi that surrounds and is directed towards the property can affect the health and finances of the occupants. Fast moving qi is not desirable so locations behind or near freeways should be avoided. Soft and hard landscaping will slow down this movement.

Intersections that are too busy are not desirable.

The owner of a home located on the outside downward curve of a steep hill may develop health problems. This energy is like a cutting blade. Planting trees to buffer this curve will protect the home. The same energy is created by the curve of a freeway.

The energy hitting a home at the end of a T street is too powerful. It is not a good location especially if the road is pointed directly at the door.

A house sitting on the inside embrace of a road will attract good energy for wealth and good health.

There is too much active energy around a house that is located with streets on the front and back. The occupants may have a hard time sleeping

6. Shape of the home

A building that is square shaped allows the energy to circulate freely. Too many angles and corners will cause stagnation

The lot shape is also important. A square is more desirable than a pie shape is desirable. The pie shape with a large facing and narrow back tends to keep the occupants from holding on to their money.

INTERIOR

1. The entry should be well lit and ventilated.

The entry is important for the flow of the energy into the house The essence of positive or negative energy enters through this opening of your home.

Any pathway leading to the entry should not be in a straight line. A curved path will soften the energy that is directed toward the door.

A planted area of shrubbery or trees will buffer and slow down this energy if it is traveling too quickly to your entrance.

2. The interior space is important to the entry. The size of the entry and door should be in proportion to the house. For example – a 30 foot ceiling can disrupt the flow of energy in the entry.

3. If a house is too large for the occupants it can feel overwhelming or lonely. Small animals like dogs or cats are good to stir up the energy in a house that feels too large for the occupants.

4. Homes with stairways that lead directly to the front door will have difficulty keeping the good "qi". The ideal solution is to slow down this energy with a plant or statue on the secondary landing or at the bottom of the steps.

In circumstances where this buffer is not possible then it is best to use another entrance and minimize the use of this door, especially if you want to improve your financial status.

5. Avoid sleeping or working for long periods of time under ceiling beams and soffits. The beams create a "sha" or negative energy over the area that it cuts across and can cause headaches or other physical problems. A soffit is a border of lowered ceiling that can run along the edge of a room.

Also a bed divided down the center by a beam can separate a couple and create the potential for relationship problems.

Soffits have the same energy as a beam and should be avoided for sleeping and working.

The outward pointing corners of a wall will also direct this energy toward your bed or desk and make the energy uncomfortable. Imagine your room like a big jacuzzi, and single jet is directed toward one area of your body for 8 hours. The energy "chi" from a sharp corner, beam or soffit will affect your body in the same manner only you are unable to see the movement of the "qi". Most people will have difficulty sitting at a desk for long periods of time with this kind of sha.

6. The energy in your home circulates and is directed through the most obvious openings, the doors. When your bed or desk is in the direct path of the doors the energy may be too direct and not so healthy. The best floor plan for a comfortable home is to position the furniture so that it is not in a direct line with the doorways. If it is not possible to move a bed out of the line of the doorways simply close the door at night.

It is best that the front door when lined up directly with the back entrance, is not open at the same time. When they are both open at the same time, it causes a tunnel effect and the positive "qi" is not retained. If this qi leaves the house, the it will be difficult for the occupant to retain wealth.

7. **Windows** are good for balancing the ventilation and light in a room. When positioning your bed it is best not sleep directly under a window unless you have proper insulation to protect the head from drafts.

8. Colors should be used with some caution if you do not know the qi layout of the building. Using red or purple in large amounts can cause an imbalance if you do not place them correctly. The color red is an activating color and can either be very good to stimulate wealth and romance, or negative and cause delays, and accidents, and arguing. Refer to the annual chart to see the direction to avoid use of the red color.

ANNUAL DIRECTIONS TO AVOID

This chart lists the directions that will bring the negative potential that causes delays in finances, accidents, conflicts, sickness etc. If your important areas such as the entry, master bedroom, children's rooms, or home office are located in these directions it is best to follow these tips-

1. Remove any objects that are very red or purple. As we mentioned earlier red/purple is a fire element and can activate the qi in a space. Fire element in a negative qi can enhance this potential harm.

2. Avoid burning a fireplace or candles in this area.

3. Add metal to the space – approximately 10-15 lbs for an average size room The metal can be decorative or not but must be a heavy mass and not covered with any other material such as plastic or rubber.

4. If you are using a water feature in this direction to enhance fame or relationships, the container should be made of metal to further reduce this negative potential.

    2006 WEST

    2007 NORTH EAST

    2008 SOUTH

    2009 NORTH

    2010 SOUTH WEST

    2011 EAST

    2012 SOUTH EAST

    2013 NORTH WEST

REORGANIZE AND SIMPLIFY-
ELIMINATE CLUTTER AND REDUCE STRESS

MAKE ROOM FOR ROMANCE

Is there room for someone new in your life?

If your home or bedroom has any of these problems its time to make a change –

1. Is your home or bedroom full of memorabilia of old relationships? Let go of the past and look forward to new opportunities. Remove or discard old letters, photos or collectibles that have bad memories.

2. Is your home cluttered with your hobbies and collectibles? If your home is completely filled it will look like you have no room for someone to share your life.

3. Does your home look and smell like a pet shop? Cat litter boxes in the bathtub and dogs in the bed can create a less than romantic odor.

Ventilate your home and check for undesirable odors. You may not notice cooking odors, pets, laundry, mildew or trash

4. Do you have stacks of magazine, newspapers and dust bunnies? Reorganizing and eliminating clutter can reduce stress.

5. Looking at a pile of stuff will give you an uneasy feeling that something is not complete. Organizing saves time and follows the feng shui principles of living life in simplicity. Keep papers and bills in a file in an area of your home or apartment that is dedicated to work.

Dealing with clutter will help you feel energized and free. Clutter can be different things-

1. mementos, photographs reminder of grievances, breakups

2. organize paperwork, file bills

3. dispose of outdated appliances, make repairs

4. update your wardrobe,

5. bathroom cabinets, for medicines, products, reminder of past illnesses

6. creating focus by eliminating clutter

7. for a more healthy environment, replace beds and linens with new ones

If it is too much to handle, hire a professional organizer. I have personally seen the results of hiring an organizer and they are worth the investment. My clients that have used an organizer have more free time, their bills are paid on time and filed and their homes are always tidy because they don't have to deal with excessive mess. Utilizing this service gives them more free time for themselves.

BEDROOMS – REST, ROMANCE AND RASPBERRIES WITH CHOCOLATE

"Enjoy life; this is not a rehearsal"

UNKNOWN

By balancing your environment and eliminating the negatives, you're taking charge of how you choose to live. Lack of sleep increases our sensitivity to stress, distorts our senses and leaves us spiritually and physically exhausted. Your bedroom should be clean and comfortable.

Tips for the making your bedroom more harmonized and balanced –

1. Place your bed in your pillow direction (see chart) page 102-109.

2. The best placement for your bed is against a solid flat wall. The energy does not circulate properly if the bed is on an angle. If you must keep your bed on angle, make sure the head is supported by a high headboard or place a screen behind the bed to support the head area.

Beds located under a window may be too drafty

3. Use colors that are supportive to enhance the energy in that direction. Neutral colors will be more restful and calming.

4. Avoid being in the direct line of a doorway. This direct path of energy while you are sleeping can disturb your sleep or health. If it is not possible relocate your bed, close the door at night.

5. Do not locate the bed under beams or overhead soffits. The qi directs itself from that beam to the part of the body that it is over. The qi current is too direct and not healthy. If you look around your room you may find some architectural feature that is causing this effect and disturbing your sleep or health. Use a tree or fabric to buffer any sharp wall corners directed at the bed.

6. Minimize the use of mirrors in the bedroom. The energy of a mirror is too "yang" (active) and any reflections that you see in the night may be disturbing to your rest.

7. Use accent lighting and avoid harsh fluorescents.

8. Eliminate distractions like computers, exercise equipment, or televisions. These items can keep you from getting your rest. A televisions is ok if you use it to keep you company on lonely nights but it is not advisable if you are looking for romance.

9. Indulge your senses with textures, aromatherapy and sounds to inspire a romantic mood. Be a little flamboyant and make your bedroom a sanctuary where you can enjoy simple pleasures like eating chocolate in bed or have an in home massage and manicure.

CHAPTER TEN
TIPS FOR IMPROVING
YOUR PERSONAL ENERGY

WHAT YOUR TRIGRAM SAYS ABOUT YOU

These characteristics of a personal trigram include the parts of the body, the 5 elements, color and direction.

People are assigned a "trigram" based on their birth date. This trigram influences a person's character and is associated with a direction. There is a different trigram for men and women born in the same year. Check the table to find your trigram then read the description of its characteristics. You can use this information to enhance your personal energy.

The trigram chart is again based on the Chinese solar calendar. The first day of the new year starts on Feb 4-5 for the Chinese solar calendar. If your birth date is for example January 20, 1980, your birth year in the Chinese calendar would be 1979 instead of 1980.

Direction

Your personal direction is the best direction for your head when you are sleeping. By placing your pillow in this direction, you will gain the best and most restful sleep

If you are studying or have a home office, the study direction is your most active and productive. Placing your desk in this direction will enhance the energy you need to be successful.

Element

Everything in the universe is composed of the one of the 5 elements. – fire, earth, metal water and wood. They are in a productive cycle because they are in a cycle where one element creates the next. Our personal trigram makes us particular to this cycle so that when we surround ourselves with elements that are productive to our particular element it will support us. When we are around too much of an element that dominates our element it can leave us feeling tired and unproductive, and may ultimately affect our well being.

Parts of the Body

According to your trigram these areas of the body may be affected by negative energy.

It doesn't mean that you will experience sickness in these areas but it will be more likely if the energy is negative in your environment.

Personality traits

Each trigram is also assigned a particular personality trait based on the family structure. It does not necessarily mean you will follow this trait but most times one will find a similarity in the personality description.

PERSONAL TRIGRAM CHART

YEAR	MALE	FEMALE	YEAR	MALE	FEMALE
1900	KAN	KEN	1926	KUN	SUN
1901	LI	CHIEN	1927	KAN	KEN
1902	KEN	TUI	1928	LI	CHIEN
1903	TUI	CHEN	1929	KEN	TUI
1904	CHIEN	LI	1930	TUI	KEN
1905	KUN	KAN	1931	CHIEN	LI
1906	SUN	KUN	1932	KUN	KAN
1907	CHEN	CHEN	1933	SUN	KUN
1908	KUN	SUN	1934	CHEN	CHEN
1909	KAN	KEN	1935	KUN	SUN
1910	LI	CHIEN	1936	KAN	KEN
1911	KEN	TUI	1937	LI	CHIEN
1912	TUI	KEN	1938	KEN	TUI
1913	CHIEN	LI	1939	TUI	KEN
1914	KUN	KAN	1940	CHIEN	LI
1915	SUN	KUN	1941	KUN	KAN
1916	CHEN	CHEN	1942	SUN	KUN
1917	KUN	SUN	1943	CHEN	CHEN
1918	KAN	KEN	1944	KUN	SUN
1919	LI	CHIEN	1945	KAN	KEN
1920	KEN	TUI	1946	LI	CHIEN
1921	TUI	KEN	1947	KEN	TUI
1922	CHIEN	LI	1948	TUI	KEN
1923	KUN	KAN	1949	CHIEN	LI
1924	SUN	KUN	1950	KUN	KAN
1925	CHEN	CHEN	1951	SUN	KUN

PERSONAL TRIGRAM CHART

YEAR	MALE	FEMALE	YEAR	MALE	FEMALE
1952	CHEN	CHEN	1977	KUN	KAN
1953	KUN	SUN	1978	SUN	KUN
1954	KAN	KEN	1979	CHEN	CHEN
1955	LI	CHIEN	1980	KUN	SUN
1956	KEN	TUI	1981	KAN	KEN
1957	TUI	KEN	1982	LI	CHIEN
1958	CHIEN	LI	1983	KEN	TUI
1959	KUN	KAN	1984	TUI	KEN
1960	SUN	KUN	1985	CHIEN	LI
1961	CHEN	CHEN	1986	KUN	KAN
1962	KUN	SUN	1987	SUN	KUN
1963	KAN	KEN	1988	CHEN	CHEN
1964	LI	CHIEN	1989	KUN	SUN
1965	KEN	TUI	1990	KAN	KEN
1966	TUI	KEN	1991	LI	CHIEN
1967	CHIEN	LI	1992	KEN	TUI
1968	KUN	KAN	1993	TUI	KEN
1969	SUN	KUN	1994	CHIEN	LI
1970	CHEN	CHEN	1995	KUN	KAN
1971	KUN	SUN	1996	SUN	KUN
1972	KAN	KEN	1997	CHEN	CHEN
1973	LI	CHIEN	1998	KUN	SUN
1974	KEN	TUI	1999	KAN	KEN
1975	TUI	KEN	2000	LI	CHIEN
1976	CHIEN	LI			

USE YOUR TRIGRAM

Quick tips to enhance your energy using your trigram information –

1. Use your pillow direction for the best rest

2. Use your study direction to place your desk for success

3. Note the parts of the body that are more vulnerable when your energy is low

4. Enhance your energy with the color or element of your trigram

PERSONAL TRIGRAM CHART

LI TRIGRAM

Direction – South

Sleeping direction – South

Desk/study direction – East

Other favorable directions – Southeast, North

Avoid these directions – Southwest, West, Northwest

Element – Fire Color – Red

Parts of the body – Eyes and heart

Illnesses – Eye and heart disease

Personality – Passionate, can be quick tempered, impulsive

PERSONAL TRIGRAM CHART

KUN TRIGRAM

Direction – Southwest

Sleeping direction – Southwest

Desk/study direction – Northeast

Other favorable directions – West, Northwest

Avoid these directions – South, Southeast, North

Element – Earth Color – Tan, Brown

Parts of the body – Stomach, reproductive area

Illnesses – digestive and reproductive problems

Personality – Motherly quality, nurturing, protective, hardworking

PERSONAL TRIGRAM CHART

TUI TRIGRAM

Direction – West

Sleeping direction – West

Desk/study direction – Northwest

Other favorable directions – Southwest, Northeast

Avoid these directions – East, Southeast, South

Element – Metal Color – White or Gold

Parts of the body – Mouth, Teeth, Chest

Illnesses – Mouth, Teeth, Chest related illnesses

Personality – Acts like the youngest member of the family, talkative, may make career from speaking (actor, lawyer)

PERSONAL TRIGRAM CHART

CHIEN TRIGRAM

Direction – Northwest

Sleeping direction – Northwest

Desk/study direction – West

Other favorable directions – Southwest, West, Northeast

Avoid these directions – South, Southeast, East, North

Element – Metal Color – White or Gold

Parts of the body – Head and Lungs

Illnesses – Head and Pulmonary diseases

Personality – Head of a business or family, president,
controlling, refined

PERSONAL TRIGRAM CHART

KAN TRIGRAM

Direction – North

Sleeping direction – North

Desk/study direction – Southeast

Other favorable directions – South, North, East

Avoid these directions – Southwest, West, Northwest, Northeast

Element – Water Color – Blue or Black

Parts of the body – Kidneys, Blood and Ears

Illnesses – Earaches and Kidney problems

Personality – Career oriented, sensitive

PERSONAL TRIGRAM CHART

KEN TRIGRAM

Direction – Northeast

Sleeping direction – Northeast

Desk/study direction – Southwest

Other favorable directions – West, Northwest

Avoid these directions – Southeast, East, North

Element – Earth Color – Tan, Yellow

Parts of the body – Hands, Fingers, Spine

Illnesses – Arthritis, Back pains

Personality – Youngest son, stubborn, loyal

PERSONAL TRIGRAM CHART

CHEN TRIGRAM

Direction – East

Sleeping direction – East

Desk/study direction – South

Other favorable directions – Southeast, North

Avoid these directions – Northeast, Northwest, West

Element – Wood Color – Green

Parts of the body – Feet, Throat

Illnesses – Hysteria, Convulsions

Personality – More emotional, represents thunder, loud, boisterous

PERSONAL TRIGRAM CHART

SUN TRIGRAM

Direction – Southeast

Sleeping direction – Southeast

Desk/study direction – North

Other favorable directions – South, North

Avoid these directions – Southwest, West, Northeast

Element – Wood Color – Green

Parts of the body – Thighs and Buttocks

Illnesses – Colds and Rheumatism

Personality – Likes to travel, adventurous, likes to lead

DOMINATING ELEMENT CHART

When your trigram element is dominated there is opposition for that element and it results in reduced energy levels and health and weakens the immune system.

Extreme amounts of the dominating element or its representing color can contribute to this effect. It can be found in your interior or exterior environment and sometimes in the clothing or accessories you wear.

Different professions can also place us in an environment with an element that may be affecting our energy levels.

Example: Profession, restaurant chef, male birthdate – May 3, 1967

Personal trigram – Chien Element – metal

Dominating element – fire

Result – being in the proximity of constant fire for 8 hours a day may diminish the energy levels resulting in increased exhaustion or health issues.

Example – Profession, metal worker, male birthdate – July 10, 1951

Personal trigram – Sun Element – wood

Dominating element – metal

Result – wearing a metal helmet/face mask to protect while welding puts metal in the proximity of the head which can result in the same reduced energy or health issues

Although clothing and jewelry are usually changed regularly they can have a small affect.

FIRE – DOMINATES – METAL

METAL – DOMINATES – WOOD

WOOD – DOMINATES – EARTH

EARTH – DOMINATES – WATER

WATER – DOMINATES – FIRE

The problem with the domination cycle can be analyzed as follows:

FIRE – melts metal

METAL – pierces, cuts wood

WOOD – roots invade the earth

EARTH – blocks flow of water

WATER – extinguishes fire

SUPPORTING ELEMENT CHART

It is often found that a person will surround themselves with the element or representing color of their trigram and supporting element. This is apparent in your interior color schemes, clothing, selection of accessories and jewelry, occupations and choice of landscape environment.(the ocean, mountains, desert, etc.)

Example – Female, birth date – August 4, 1955

Personal trigram – Chien   Element – metal

Supporting element – earth

Results – clothing choices may be white, neutrals, interior color selections may be neutrals, whites, gold, silver

Jewelry choices – metal, gold, silver

Using supportive colors she can include tans, yellows

Example – Male, birth date – December 22, 1973

Personal trigram – Kan Element – water

Supporting element – metal

Results – clothing may be blue, black, interior color selections may be blue, black

Using supporting colors he can include white, neutrals, gold, and silver

The supporting element is the element that produces the next element.

FIRE – PRODUCES – EARTH

EARTH – PRODUCES – METAL

METAL – PRODUCES – WATER

WATER – PRODUCES – WOOD

WOOD – PRODUCES – FIRE

CHAPTER ELEVEN
PUTTING IT ALL TOGETHER

NEW CONFIDENCE

Once you try this method to find romance you will most likely feel much more confident and have more self esteem. Why not? After all someone will be choosing you! You will be noticed and sought after and you will increase your chances to find that perfect relationship because suddenly you have more options. Hopefully, you have followed the advice in this book and have not only improved your self image but have made your environment more healthy and added more fun in your life. The simple fact that you are more desirable is exciting. This can be the beginning of a new you!

Try a makeover – to renew your inner and outer energy, start a self discovery to new relationships and choose a different path.

Have fun with a new look, different hairstyle, color and makeup.

Experiment with a new wardrobe, perhaps a professional can help you choose the styles that will reflect the best qualities of your figure. Be open for change to accompany your new experiences. Confidence is real attractive. Since the peach blossom energy attraction is random your positive outlook is sure to bring you more prospective relationships.

Eliminating clutter from the past or updating your appearance can be an uplifting and reenergizing. Check your trigram elements and accentuate your surrounding with the colors that support your personal energy.

CHECK LIST FOR ROMANCE

1. Use the flowers/vase in proper direction

2. Identify the directions that will help enhance fame and romance with water

3. Balance your environment, exterior and interior

4. Be accessible – change your routine and surroundings

5. Make a "wish" list to find the person best for "you"

6. Use your element colors and supporting colors to energize

7. Make your bedroom a sanctuary to sleep and get reenergized

8. Begin now!

Luckily I was introduced to the peach blossom formula in my feng shui studies with Master Sang. I am most grateful for his knowledge and for the effort he has made to make this information available to his students. I have attempted to update this ancient knowledge to make it useful for today's relationships. The ancient principles are the same but the steps to enhancing the newfound relationship is for our new world of dating.

I hope that this little bit of feng shui knowledge will enlighten my readers to follow their hearts and live for today. If the flowers do nothing else but make you feel that you are alive and special, then I've fulfilled my dream.

Janice Sugita has been my student for many years and due to her hard work, has also become one of my instructors. She has shown great initiative in applying Feng Shui. From this, she has improved her own life and the lives of many of her students, clients, friends, and family. This book is the result of her experimentation with my 'peach blossom' technique. I am sure it will benefit the readers as well, and bring them good relationships and the chance to meet a loving spouse.

Master Larry Sang, Founder
American Feng Shui Institute

DISCLAIMER

The author of this book makes no representation or warranties with respect to the accuracy or content of this material. The author shall in no way be held liable for any loss or damages and the reader should use this book as a general guide at their own discretion. The application of the material is totally the readers responsibility.